AWESOME ATHLETES

MICHAEL JORDAN

Paul Joseph
ABDO & Daughters

Published by Abdo & Daughters, 4940 Viking Drive, Suite 622, Edina, Minnesota 55435.

Copyright © 1997 by Abdo Consulting Group, Inc., Pentagon Tower, P.O. Box 36036, Minneapolis, Minnesota 55435 USA. International copyrights reserved in all countries. No part of this book may be reproduced in any form without written permission from the publisher.

Printed in the United States.

Cover and Interior Photo credits: Wide World Photos
Allsport USA

Edited by Kal Gronvall

Library of Congress Cataloging-in-Publication Data

Joseph, Paul, 1970-
Michael Jordan / Paul Joseph; [edited by Kal Gronvall].
p. cm. — (Awesome athletes)
Includes index.
Summary: Describes the life and basketball career of the high-scoring player who led the Chicago Bulls to four NBA championships.
ISBN 1-56239-641-2
1. Jordan, Michael, 1963- --Juvenile literature. 2. Basketball players—United States—Biography—Juvenile literature. 3. Chicago Bulls (Basketball team)—Juvenile literature. [1. Jordan, Michael, 1963- . 2. Basketball players. 3. Afro-Americans—Biography.]
I. Gronvall, Kal. II. Title. III. Series.
GV884.J67J66 1997
796.323'092—dc20
[B]   96-27215
                                                                       CIP
                                                                        AC

Contents

The Greatest Basketball Player Ever

Michael Jordan is easily the greatest basketball player in the history of the game. He has accomplished more than any other player. He has succeeded both individually, and—more important to Michael—as a team member.

In high school, Michael led his team to a state **championship**. In college he led his team to an **NCAA** title, won the Player of the Year Award, and received a gold medal playing in the **Olympics** for the United States.

Those awards were only the beginning. He didn't really begin to shine until he got into the **National Basketball Association (NBA)**, where he continues to dominate.

Chicago Bulls' Michael Jordan drives to the hoop.

In Michael's first year in the NBA he received the **Rookie of the Year** Award. In 1986, he started his string of seven-straight **scoring titles**. In 1988, he showed that he can also play defense, picking up the **Defensive Player of the Year** Award, with a **record** number of steals.

In 1991, he led his Chicago Bulls to an NBA **Championship**—their first of three in a row! In all three championships, he was named **Most Valuable Player (MVP)**. After the third NBA title, Michael surprised everyone by **retiring** from the game he loved.

Michael returned in the second half of the 1995 season. By 1996, he was his old self again, leading the Bulls to a fourth NBA title while earning his fourth Finals MVP, his fourth league MVP, and his eighth scoring title!

Michael has proven many times that he is the greatest player in the history of basketball. But getting there was a long and difficult struggle, filled with many hours of practice. Believe it or not, Michael was **cut** from his high school basketball team the first time he tried out.

Michael Jordan after the 1991 NBA Finals.

A Country Boy From Carolina

Michael Jeffrey Jordan was born February 17, 1963, in Brooklyn, New York. Shortly thereafter, his family moved to Wilmington, North Carolina.

His father, James, worked as a **mechanic** at an electric plant. His mother, Deloris, worked in customer service at a local bank. Michael has two older brothers, James and Larry, an older sister, Deloris, and a younger sister, Roslyn.

While growing up, Michael had family, sports, and friends. His parents and siblings gave him a lot of support and **companionship**. His parents always stressed to Michael the importance of being honest and working hard at whatever he did.

Michael loved living in the rural area of North Carolina. He enjoyed the peaceful, small-town atmosphere. To this day, Michael remembers his roots and calls himself "a country boy from Carolina."

Michael's first true love was baseball—not basketball. In little league, Michael was the star pitcher. Many believed he was the best on the team. When Michael dreamed about playing **professional** sports it was baseball he dreamed about, not basketball.

Then his older brother Larry got him interested in basketball. Larry played him one-on-one and beat him badly. Michael was determined to work hard and beat his older brother. They usually played two hours a day and all day on weekends. Michael was so determined to be a great basketball player that he would even pay his sisters and neighbor kids to do his chores so he could continue practicing and playing.

Michael eventually got to be a great basketball player and could even beat his brother. By the time he entered high school he was an excellent all-around **athlete**. He played outfield and pitched for the baseball team. He played quarterback in football. And he played guard on the basketball team.

Heartbreak and Joy

Michael believed he was ready to be on the **varsity** basketball team in his second year of high school. But after the tryouts were completed, Michael was **cut**—he didn't make the team. Michael was heartbroken. The coach believed that Michael would do better playing on the junior varsity team where he would have more playing time, and a year to grow.

Michael was determined to prove his coach wrong. He continued to practice day and night. He was so into basketball that he forgot about school. Michael would skip classes to practice basketball. After his parents found out that he was skipping school they punished him and told him that an education is the most important thing in his life.

Michael's main goal was to go to college, and he knew that he couldn't do that without good grades in school. So Michael began a routine where he would divide his time between basketball and school work. It paid off. He had a B-average in school and made the **varsity** team his junior year.

Michael played great basketball, and by the time he reached his senior year he was a star. Michael averaged 23 points per game and broke all of his school's scoring **records**. People came just to watch him. The games began at 7:30 P.M. The gym was packed by 5:30 P.M.

Michael led his high school team to a State **Championship** title. Colleges were starting to call on Michael, hoping he would go to their school.

A North Carolina Tar Heel

Michael chose the University of North Carolina (UNC). UNC had a great basketball tradition as well as many talented players on their team. Michael was very excited. He received a full basketball **scholarship**. Michael was happy that he was staying in his home state to go to college.

Michael credited his parents for his college success. They not only stressed the importance of education, but they also taught him right from wrong.

Many people in his hometown thought that Michael would sit on the bench in college—at least his first two years. Michael didn't know what to expect. He walked in his first day of practice and saw James Worthy and Sam Perkins—two future NBA stars—and was a little intimidated.

But Michael continued his usual hard work ethic, practicing more than anyone else on the team. Michael was always the first at practice and the last one to leave. And in his spare time he would play pickup games.

Michael quickly impressed his coach, Dean Smith, who made him a starter. Coach Smith was known throughout the country for not starting **freshmen**, but Michael was the exception.

Michael quickly proved that he deserved to be in the starting lineup. In the first home game Michael scored 22 points and grabbed 5 rebounds. Michael helped the Tar Heels jump-start to a 10-0 **record** and the Number One ranking in the nation.

Michael Jordan drives past an Indiana opponent.

"The Shot"

North Carolina kept up that Number One ranking throughout the year, finishing the season with an outstanding 27-2 **record**. Michael finished with a 13.5 scoring average, and was named the Atlantic Coast Conference **Rookie of the Year**.

But what mattered most to Michael was that his team was heading to the **NCAA** tournament. The winner of this tournament would be considered the best college team in the country.

The Tar Heels strolled through the tournament all the way to the **championship** game. There, they met the Georgetown Hoyas, who were led by Patrick Ewing—the best center in the game.

The contest was tight throughout, with many lead changes. In fact, no team ever led by more than six points. With less than a minute left in the game, the Hoyas took a 62-61 lead.

With only 18 seconds remaining, Michael took a pass from a teammate, and quickly put up a 16-foot jump shot. He hit nothing but net, giving the Tar Heels a one-point lead.

The Hoyas had one last chance but turned the ball over. The North Carolina Tar Heels were the 1982 National Champions. And Michael Jordan became a household name, thanks to what became known as "The Shot."

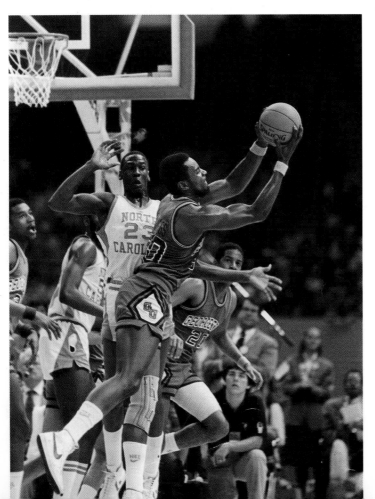

Michael Jordan (23) defends against the Georgetown Hoyas.

THE MAKING OF AN AWESOME ATHLETE

Michael Jordan celebrates another world championship with his family.

1963	1982	1984	1985
Born February 17 in Brooklyn, New York.	Helps the North Carolina Tar Heels become National Champions.	Drafted No. 3 by the NBA's Chicago Bulls.	Named the NBA's Rookie of the Year.

How Awesome Is He?

There have been many high scorers in the NBA, but only a few handled the ball and hit the boards as well as Jordan.

	Avg. Pts.	Avg. Asst.	Avg. Reb.
Michael Jordan	**32.2**	**5.9**	**6.3**
Charles Barkley	23.3	3.9	11.6
Larry Bird	24.3	6.3	10.0
Wilt Chamberlain	30.1	4.4	22.9
Magic Johnson	19.7	11.4	7.3
Hakeem Olajuwon	23.7	2.5	12.5

MICHAEL JORDAN

TEAM: CHICAGO BULLS
NUMBER: 23 & 45
POSITION: GUARD
HEIGHT: 6 FEET 6 INCHES
WEIGHT: 200 LBS.

1987

Wins first of seven-consecutive NBA scoring titles.

1993

Leads the Bulls to their third-straight NBA Championship; announces retirement.

1995

Returns to the NBA in March; leads the Bulls to the playoffs.

1996

Wins his eighth NBA scoring title; named NBA and Finals MVP.

- 2-Time All-American & NCAA Player of the Year
- 2-Time Olympic Gold Medalist
- 1985 NBA Rookie of the Year
- 8-Time NBA Scoring Champion
- 4-Time NBA MVP
- 4-Time NBA Champion and Finals MVP
- 10-Time NBA All-Star Selection
- 1988 NBA Defensive Player of the Year

Highlights

A Jump to the NBA

Everywhere Michael went people wanted his **autograph** and to talk about "The Shot," but Michael just wanted to play ball. In his **sophomore** year Michael averaged 20 points a game and led his team to 28 wins. But in the **NCAA** tournament the Tar Heels were quickly eliminated. Despite the loss, Jordan was named **College Player of the Year**.

The following year Jordan led his team to another impressive **record**, finishing 28-3. Michael led his team and the conference in scoring, and again was named Player of the Year.

Many believed that the Tar Heels were the best team in the country and would easily win a second **championship**. But Indiana upset North Carolina in the semifinals, leaving Michael very disappointed.

Michael started to get restless playing college ball. Teams were double- and triple-teaming him. In addition, the media was hounding him, and he had accomplished everything he could at the college level. Michael decided to leave school early and join the NBA.

As with every important decision in his life, Michael discussed the issue with his parents. His parents supported his decision to leave college early and join the NBA, but they still wanted him to someday finish college. Michael promised his parents that he would take summer classes until he **graduated**, which he did. Two years after he left for the NBA, Michael graduated from college.

On May 5, 1984, Michael Jordan made the official announcement that he was leaving the University of North Carolina to play **professional** basketball.

On his birthday, Jordan serves his mother and father a slice of cake.

A Gold Medal and Rookie of the Year

Michael Jordan was the third player chosen in the 1984 NBA **draft**. The lucky team that got him was the Chicago Bulls. But before Michael joined the Bulls he represented his country in the 1984 Summer **Olympics**. Jordan helped the United States win a gold medal.

Now it was time for the NBA. Michael got off to a quick start, dazzling the fans with his high-flying dunks and scoring ability. Michael scored 25 or more points in 10 of first 15 games.

Michael was an instant sensation. Even on the road people would come to watch him. In 1984, Michael led the Bulls—who were horrible the year before he arrived—to the **playoffs**.

Michael finished the season with a 28.2 scoring average and **Rookie of the Year** honors. Although the

Bulls were quickly ousted from the **playoffs**, the fans knew that someday Michael would lead them to a **championship**.

In 1985, Michael didn't get to play much basketball. During the third game of the season, Michael broke his foot and didn't return until the end of the season.

But in 1986, Michael came out and totally dominated the league. In his first game he scored 50 points and followed that up with 41 points the next game. He finished the season with a 37.1 average and his first of seven-straight **scoring titles**. Only the great Wilt Chamberlain has had a higher single-season average.

Michael was also the first player to have over 200 steals and 100 blocked shots in a season. However, in the playoffs the Bulls were easily eliminated.

Building a Championship Team

Besides Michael, the Bulls didn't have many good players. In 1987, the team signed Scottie Pippen, who would help Michael build the Bulls into a **dynasty**. Michael was happy because now all of the load was not on his shoulders.

Michael proved he was just as dominant on defense as he was on offense. He won the **Defensive Player of the Year** Award, the **MVP** Award, and another **scoring title**.

Michael, along with Pippen, led his team to the **playoffs** where they picked up their first series win. In the next round the Bulls were knocked off by the highly-favored Detroit Pistons.

In the 1988-89 season, Michael again won the scoring crown. More important, the Bulls were getting much better. In the playoffs they surprised many by getting to the Eastern Conference **Championship**. Again they lost to the Pistons, who went on to win the NBA title.

The following year the same thing happened. But everyone knew that the Bulls had built a great team, and for the next three years they would prove it.

Michael Jordan, planning his next move against Dan Majerle and the Phoenix Suns in the NBA finals.

Three-peat

In the 1990-91 season, the Bulls put it all together and raced to an NBA **Championship** season. After building the team around Michael Jordan, patience finally paid off.

Of course Michael led the way, having another unbelievable season. He won another **scoring title**, was the league **MVP** and the NBA Finals MVP. What more could Michael accomplish? Many thought nothing, but he did even better the next year.

In the 1991-92 season, Michael again led his team to an NBA Championship, won a scoring title, earned league and Finals MVP awards—and won another **Olympic** gold medal! After winning the NBA Championship, Michael joined other NBA stars and represented his country for a second time as part of the original "Dream Team."

Experts believed that Michael couldn't lead the Bulls to a third-consecutive championship. Magic Johnson didn't do it, Larry Bird didn't do it, and Isiah Thomas didn't do it.

Only one other team in history had done it and that was nearly 30 years earlier. But don't ever count Michael out.

Michael led his team to the NBA Finals, where he set a **record** with an incredible 43-points-per-game average! The Bulls captured their third-straight title and Michael received his third Finals **MVP**. The fans got to see a team **three-peat**.

Michael had done it all. There was nothing more to accomplish. In October 1993, Michael shocked basketball fans everywhere by **retiring** from basketball.

Michael was happy that his father got to see him play his last game. Less than a month later, tragedy struck. James Jordan was murdered. It left Michael with an empty feeling. James had been Michael's best friend and supporter. And he attended most of Michael's **professional** games.

Even more, Michael's dad had taught him about life and how to be a good human being. "My dad taught me to carry myself with love and respect for all."

"I'm Back"

When the 1993-94 basketball season started, Michael was not around. He took some time off, thought about his father, and spent quality time with his family.

Michael even followed his childhood dream and tried playing **professional** baseball. Although it didn't go as well as he had planned, he did enjoy swinging the bat and playing the outfield again.

Michael also liked the fact that he was no longer in the limelight. One thing was missing for Michael, and that was basketball. He started playing basketball just for fun. Then he began going to UNC and Bulls' practices.

In March 1995 Michael issued a two-word press release that read: "I'm back." In his first game, Michael was his usual self, scoring 55 points!

But the Bulls never really got on track. They won in the first round of the **playoffs** before falling to the Orlando Magic. But fans were just glad Michael was back.

Michael Jordan playing for the Chicago White Sox minor league team.

He's Really Back!

In 1995-96, Michael played his first full season since his short **retirement**. His comeback was awesome. Michael won his eighth **scoring title**, his fourth league **MVP**, and led the Bulls to their fourth NBA **Championship**. Michael even picked up another Finals MVP Award.

Besides winning individual awards, Michael also is a great team leader. Besides dominating offensively, he prides himself more on his spectacular defense. And besides being head-and-shoulders above the rest on the court, he is even better off the court.

Despite his busy schedule, he always has time for children and **charities**. He has set up the Michael Jordan Foundation that gives back to the community. He also invites children to most of his games and meets with them after he is done playing.

He is a big supporter of the Ronald McDonald houses. And his presence at **charity** events has brought in hundreds of thousands of dollars.

Because family means so much to Michael he founded and funded the James Jordan Boys and Girls Club and Family Life Center in Chicago, named after his father. It will help provide a healthy environment for children, teenagers, and their parents.

Michael Jordan holds his daughter Jasmine while his wife Juanita and sons Marcus and Jeffrey look on.

There is nothing more on the basketball court for Michael to accomplish. He will easily be elected to the Hall of Fame and will surely be remembered as the greatest basketball player of all time.

Besides all that, Michael will be remembered as a great guy. Bill Russell, the great Boston Celtic center, once said that Michael was an even better human being than he was a basketball player. That may be the greatest tribute of all.

29

Glossary

athlete - Someone who is physically skilled and talented at sports.

autograph - A signature of someone famous.

championship - The final basketball game or series, to determine the best team.

charities - A fund or organization for helping the poor, the sick, and the helpless.

College Player of the Year - An award given to the best college basketball player in the nation.

companionship - Someone who is there to keep you company.

cut - Trying out for a team and then not making it.

Defensive Player of the Year - The best player on defense in a particular year.

draft - An event held where NBA teams choose amateur players to be on their team. After the lottery teams pick, it then goes according to team record with the best team getting the last pick.

dynasty - A great team for many years.

freshman - A first-year college student.

graduate - Finishing a certain school and getting your diploma.

junior varsity - The second-best team in high school or college sports.

mechanic - A person skilled at working with tools, especially someone who repairs machines.

Most Valuable Player (MVP) - An award given to the best player in the league, All-Star Game, or NBA Finals.

National Basketball Association (NBA) - A professional basketball league in the United States and Canada consisting of the Eastern and Western Conference.

NCAA - This stands for the National Collegiate Athletic Association, which oversees all athletic competition at the college level.

Olympics - Athletic contests held every four years in a different country. Athletes from many nations compete in them.

playoffs - Games played by the best teams after the regular season to determine a champion.

professional - Playing a sport and getting paid for it.

record - The best it has ever been done in a certain event. Also, the count of wins and losses by a team.

retire - Quitting a profession or job after many years on your own terms.

rookie - A first-year player in a sport.

Rookie of the Year - An award given to the best rookie player in that particular year.

scholarship - A money award used to pay for school given to people for their particular skills.

scoring title - An award given to the player who averages the most points per game for an entire season.

sophomore - A second-year college student.

three-peat - Winning three championships in a row.

varsity - The best team in high school or college sports.

Index